Brian Rider

Mini Guide
Axonometric &
Isometric drawing

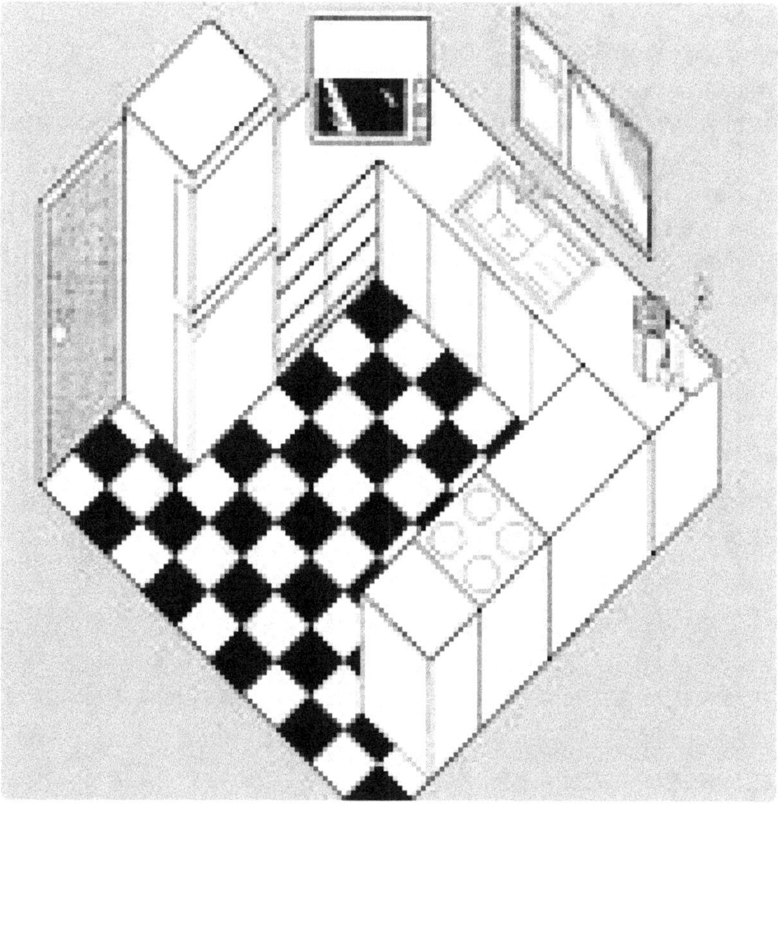

Foreword

Thank you for choosing one of our New
Mini Guides. The purpose of these guides
is to provide a simple paperback training
guide in a variety of KBB and Interior
Designer or even Exterior Designer titles
which extract the highly focussed
information from our giant tomes that ran
about 1000 pages and which would cost a
lot more than you would wish to pay or we
would wish to charge, With our mini
guides you can acquire any of the titles at
an extremely modes targeted sum.

1

COPYRIGHT

©century 21 publishing 2016

2

Axonometric method

"The simplest of all 3d methods"

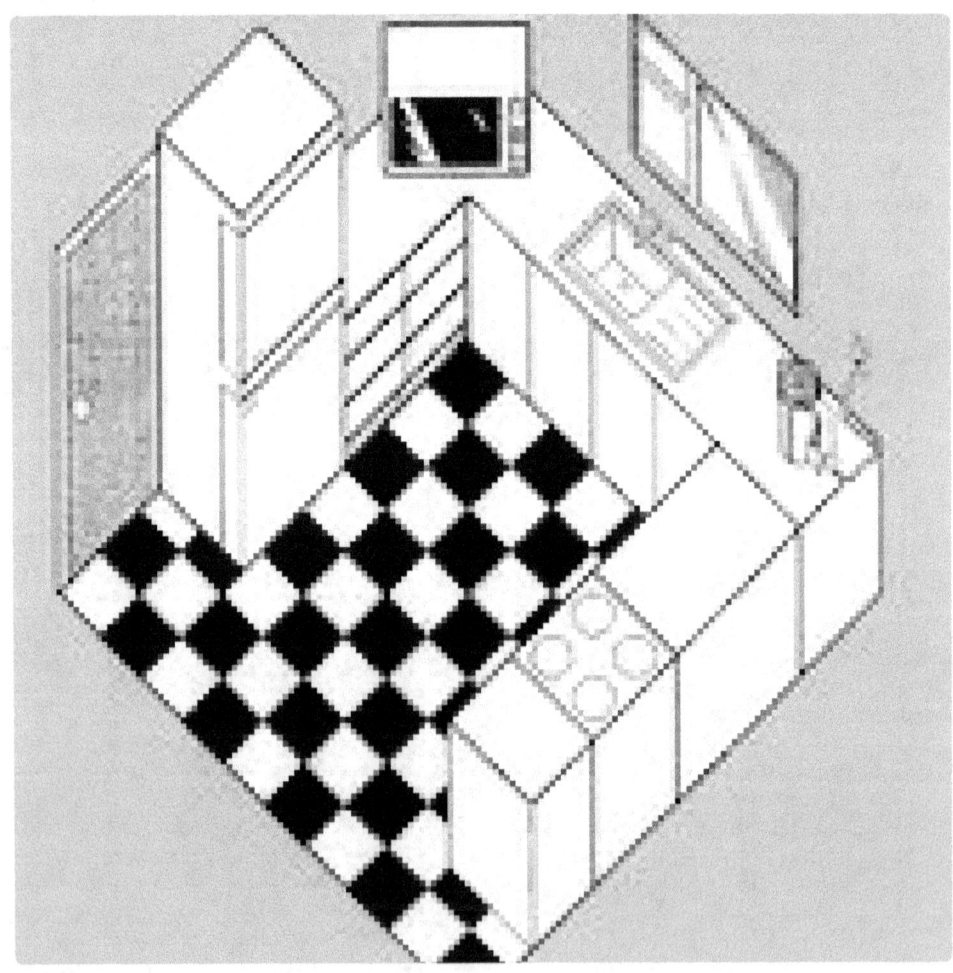

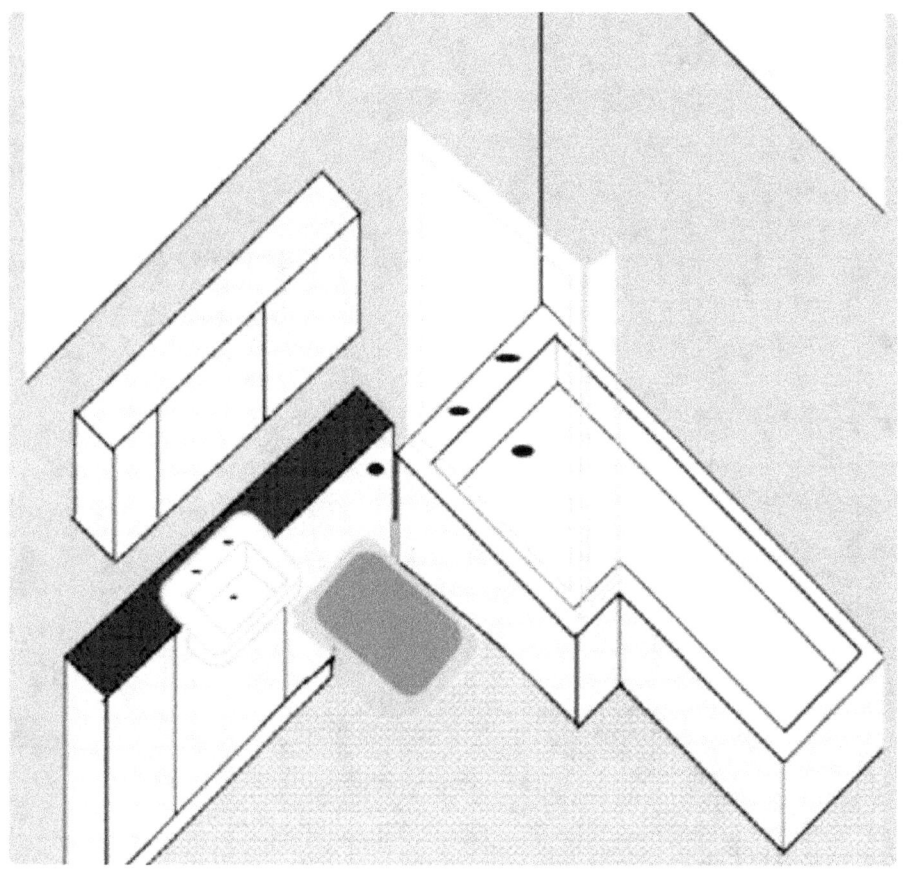

This is a very simple technique using the 45° set square. As it is symmetrical it is easier to follow without getting confused. It also produces a better drawing, for example in Bathrooms where the view is fairly balanced

Step by Step

Start with a Scale Plan

This is our starting plan

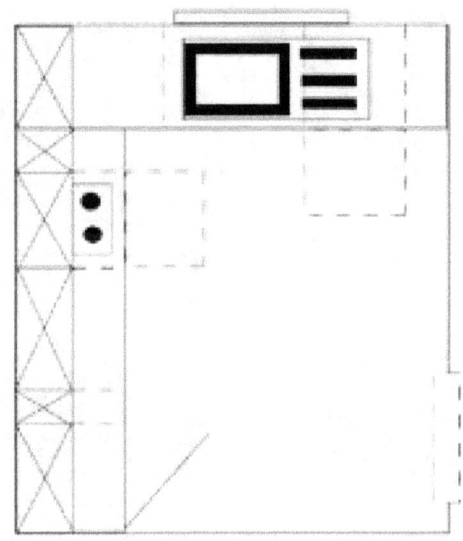

REMEMBER

1. Axonometric is not particularly suitable for kitchens but it is an excellent tool for preparing a service plan and/or a survey

2. always remember to use your drawing board

3. all vertical lines should be square

4. all working lines should be 45°

The axonometric drawing is a very useful and simple technique to product a pleasing 3d effect using only a drawing board and a 45° set square. As with all of these methods we recommend starting with a scale plan to ensure that the 3d can be produced quickly and accurately. It you were drawing a kitchen. for example. you would find the corner of the room as in an L shape kitchen and mark off the unit sizes. If you do not know the actual unit sizes you can use the default size of 2m height for tall units or wall units, 900 high for base units, 600 deep for base and tall units and 300 deep for wall units. Wall unit heights can vary but use the set out dimension of 2m and then use an arbitrary 600 or 700 height of wall unit.

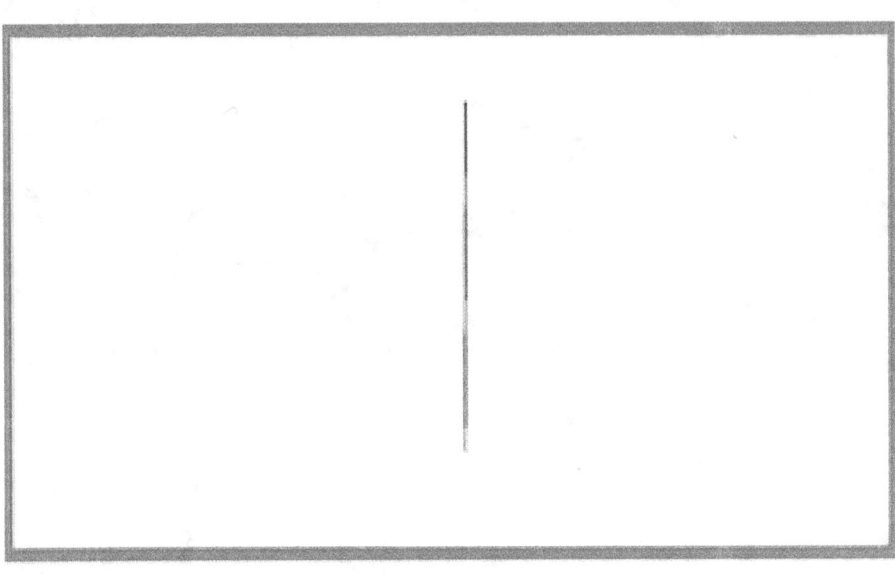

Step by Step

draw the back corner of the room at the centre of the units positioned on left and right hand walls.

Default height is 2400mm

In all cases use the actual dimensions of the units you are drawing if known.

As with all drawings you start with the drawing board and set square   Remember to use portrait or landscape whichever is more appropriate.

Let us assume that the ceiling height is a standard 2.4 metres and the length of the two walls are 2 metres by 3 metres. Your starter drawing would therefore be as follows .

Just to remind you of the basic drawing please see the following step by step guide.

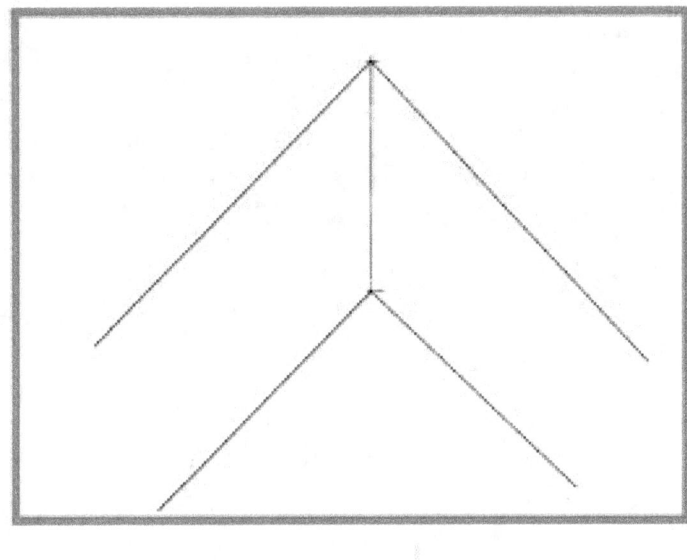

Step by Step

At the floor and ceiling points using your
45° set square draw 2 lines left and right
to show the left and right hand walls

If you wish you can use just a sheet of paper a sturdy ruler and a set square.

Just make sure that you hold the paper and the rulers and set square steady and use light strokes when you draw. Also remember that you will be removing many lines as the drawing progresses so the lighter the better and then you can use a heavier pencil later,

For those o f you that have chosen a computer drawing method, you will find that you can select a very faint line to beg inand then remove those lines or replace the lines that are in the way and then change the weight of the line later - in fact it is childishly simple

on virtually any drawing programme.

To produce an accurate drawing you should also be using a scale ruler but if you do not want to invest in such an item you can use an ordinary ruler and the standard scale of 1:20 i.e. every 1 cm or mm equal 20. You could also use a marking pen to note some of the more commonly used conversion on your cheap wood ruler. i.e. 600mm 1 metre etc.

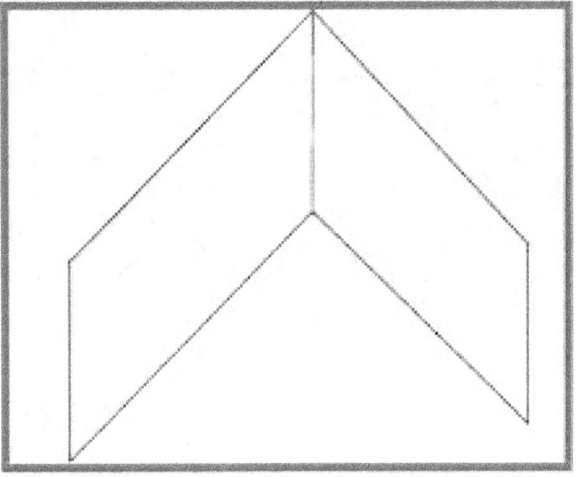

Using your scale plan measure each wall
and finish each wall with a vertical line at
the end.

Once you have produced your basic room outline just pause for a moment to check that have actually produced the right size and shape. Errors at this stage will be compounded at later stages when you start to add detail.

However, I am sure you will want to produce these drawings in the minimum possible time and perhaps spend a little more time on final presentation. If you are using the drawing to sell a project this can be a valuable stage.

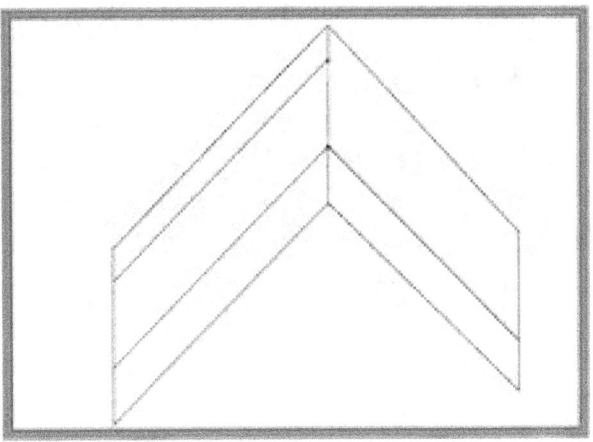

Step by Step

Now mark off the height of the base units and the height of the wall units. note that there are only wall units on the left hand wall. Use your own range measurements or use the standard default of 90mm for base units and 2115 to top of wall units to accommodate 715 wall units.

You can also use 2m ceiling height to accommodate 600 high wall units.

We are now getting through to the detail stage so make sure you are using the correct measurements..

We have suggested simple default measurements but in all cases use your own measurements if you have a specific product you are regularly using or if you wish to translate the technique to another type of interior drawing such as a living room or bedroom. Basically it is all the same technique and just the sizes vary.

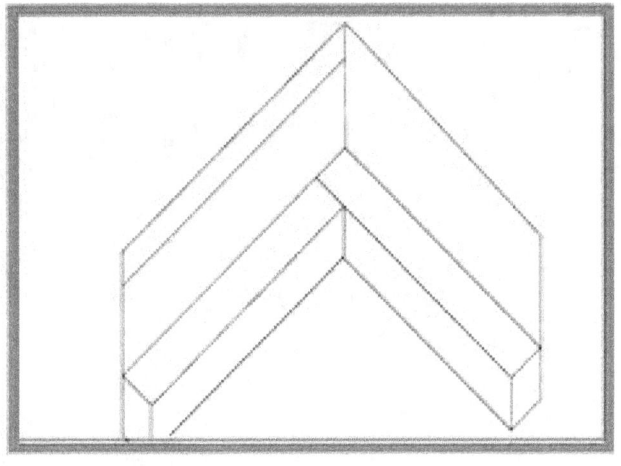

Step by Step

Again using your 45ª set square at the end of each base line project 2 lines at the top and bottom of the base line and measure out the depth of 600mm, the default carcasse depth.

The drawing is now beginning to take shape and you will find that some of the lines are interfering with your view of the drawing. This is particularly important when you first start drawing as it is more difficult to SEE the actual shapes taking place because of the confusion of the different overlapping lines.

As you progress with the drawing you can remove any lines that will not be required for further detail such as the floor lines which by now will probably be totally hidden. But remember only to remove the lines or parts of the lines that are not required for the final drawing.

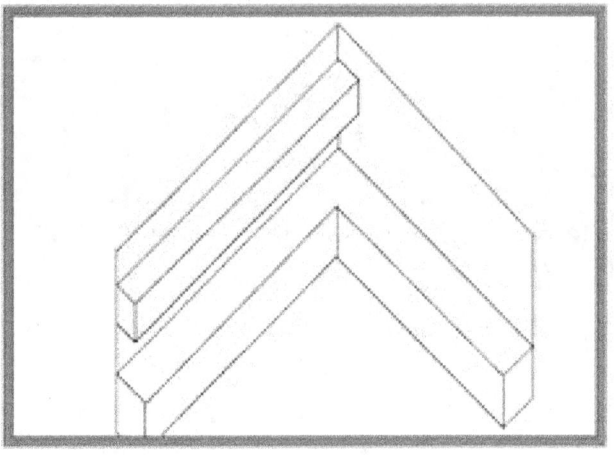

Step by Step Step 6

Repeat this step for the wall line using the default measurement of 715mm height and 300mm depth

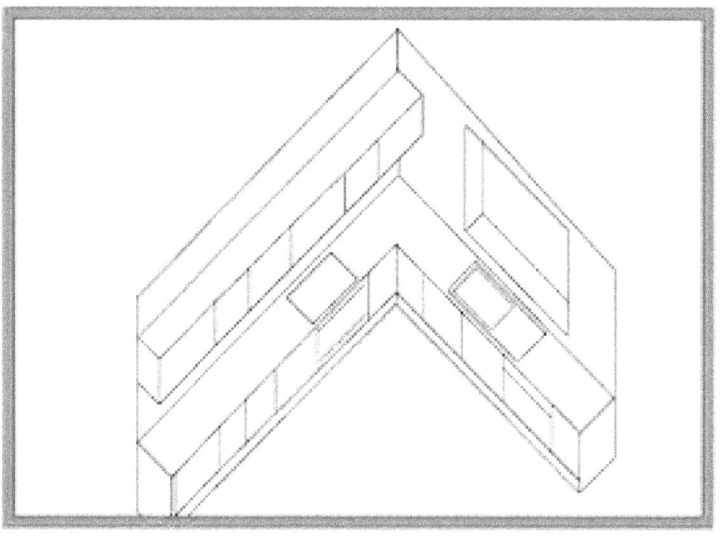

Step by Step

Mark off the individual wall and base units using your scale plan and ruler and define each unit with a vertical line

You can also start adding features such as the hob and sink just by using 45° parallel lines.

We have now made excellent progress and you can see the final drawing emerging.

The extent of the detail in the drawing really depends on the project and how much detail would be desirable.

You can add worktop thickness, plilnth inset, even the inset of appliance detail but ask yourself "is it worth it?" does the extra time and effort really make that much Saleable detail. Try a few you will soon be able to use your judgment for that particular project of possibly the client or customer.

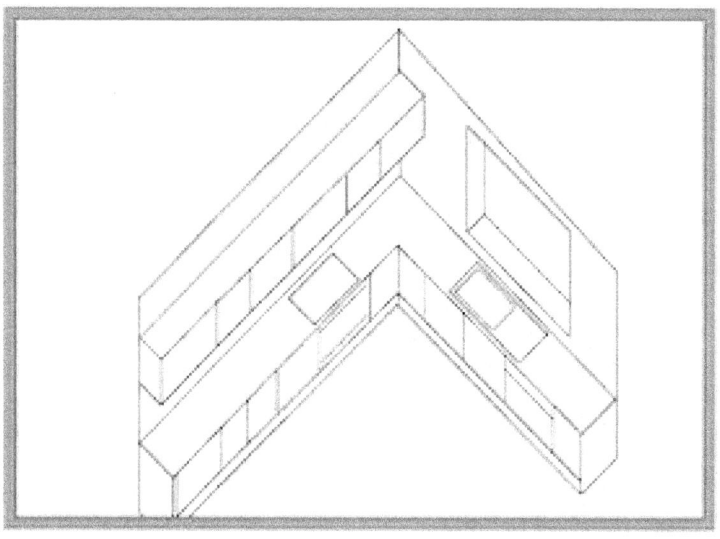

Step by Step

At this stage we have also added the window and the depth of the window again just using 45 parallel lines.

We can also add other features such as the worktop thickness, the plinth inset and any open shelves or glazed units

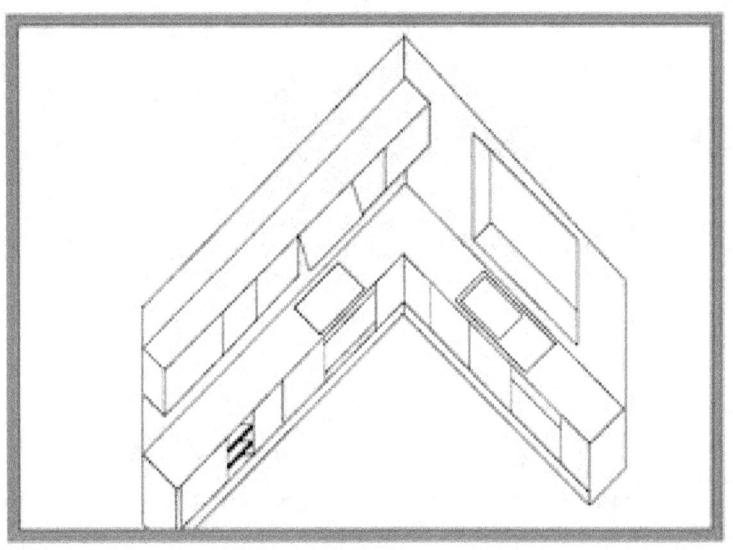

Step by Step   Step 9

Note the plinth height in this stage and the open shelf. Default plinth height is 150mm

We are also showing the cooker hood door open. You would normally use a shallower angle - 30^a is quite useful.

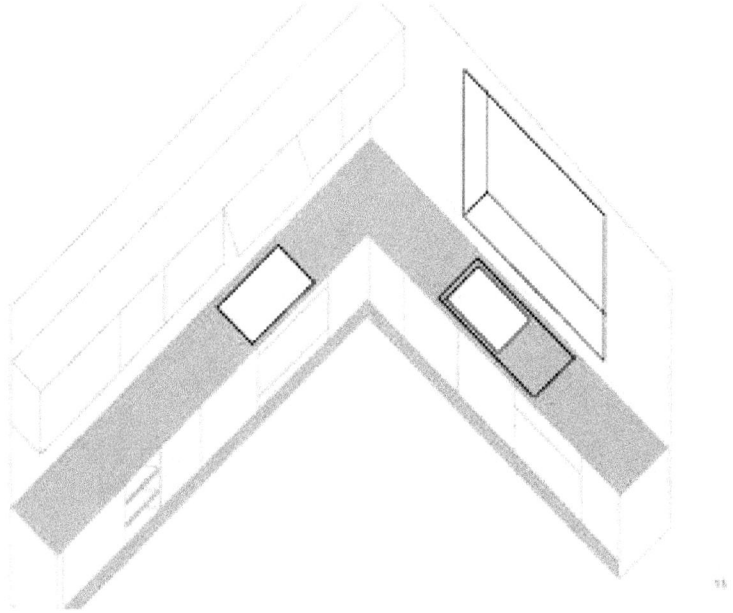

Final drawing with a touch of rendering which you can also complete in colour and or textures.

The Axonometric
Drawing

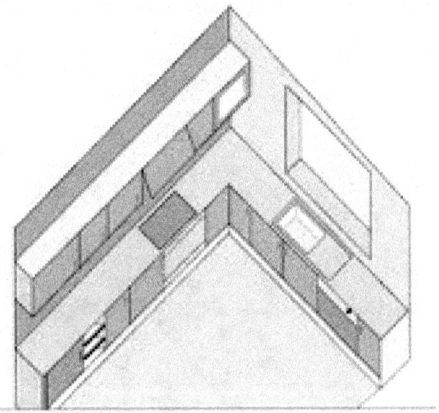

Another rendered drawing also please note the sink depth again using vertical and 45ª parallel lines

OK we have reached the end, completion is in the eye of the beholder

It is important to add some rendering but exactly what rendering will depend again on your own judgment of the project and or the client.

This is a monochrome guide so we are showing monochrome rendering. If you are producing copies this maybe your desired answer especially with the cost of ink if you are using a computer,but , equally, producing a colour rendered drawing is so easy. especially on a computer. Even if you did draw by hand you might even find that scanning your drawing for the final rendering may be the easiest solution but equally, if you have enjoyed the drawing process which so many people do, you may wish to use your own skills to render the final drawing.

If you are using a computer process rendering will be available within the drawing programme or via a separate graphic programme such as Graphic Converter. The variation of colours and patterns is quite remarkable.

Ideal method for room
interiors such as
kitchens and bedrooms

3

ISOMETRIC
METHOD

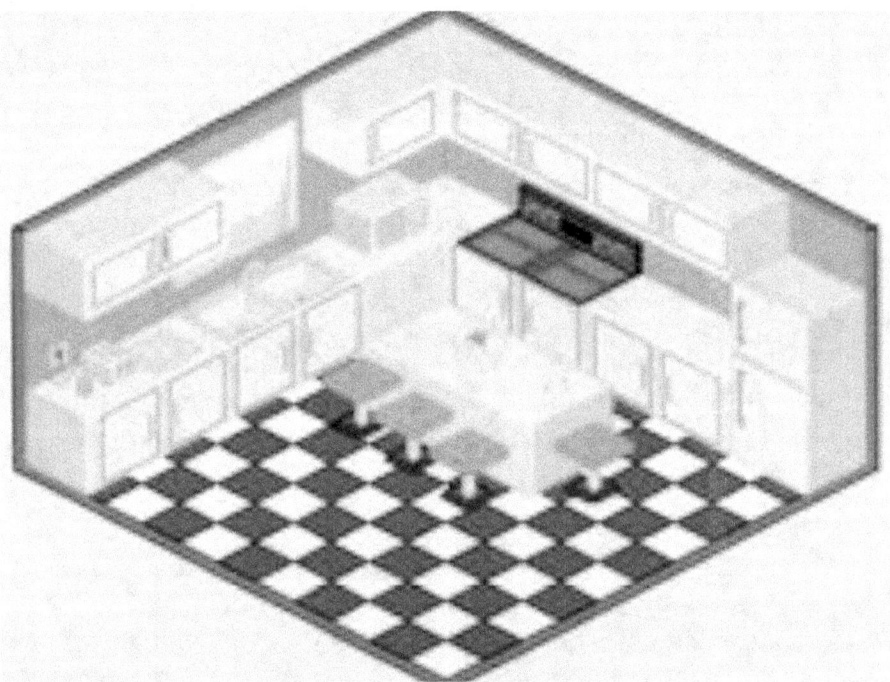

THE ISOMETRIC METHOD often referred to as PLAN A METRIC, is virtually the same method but uses a 30°/60° set square and alternate use of these 2 angles although generally it is 30° for the width and 60° for the depth. Height is drawn at 90° as normal

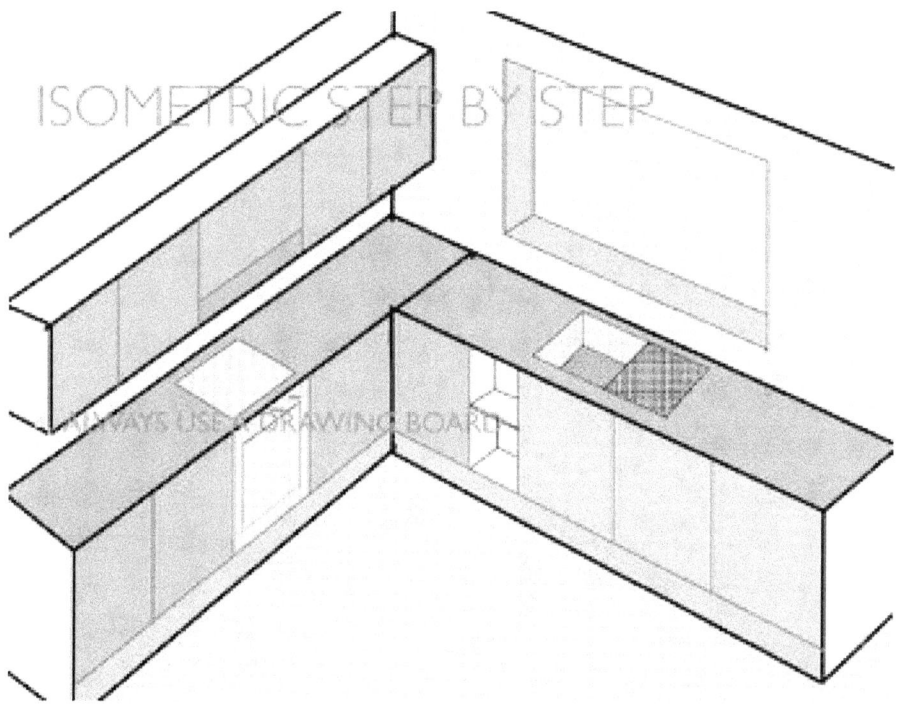

The method is basically the same as the Axonometric using the fixed angles for parallel perspective drawing.

As before start with a scale plan. If you haven't got one, make one using the Axon example as a guide

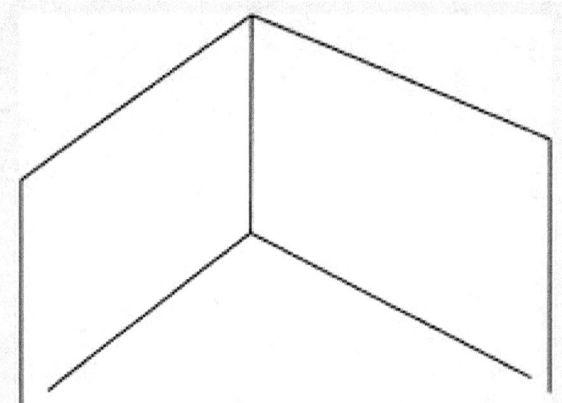

STEP 1 - THE ROOM SIZE IN SCALE

draw the 2 or possibly 3 walls that have significant context - use 1:20 scale

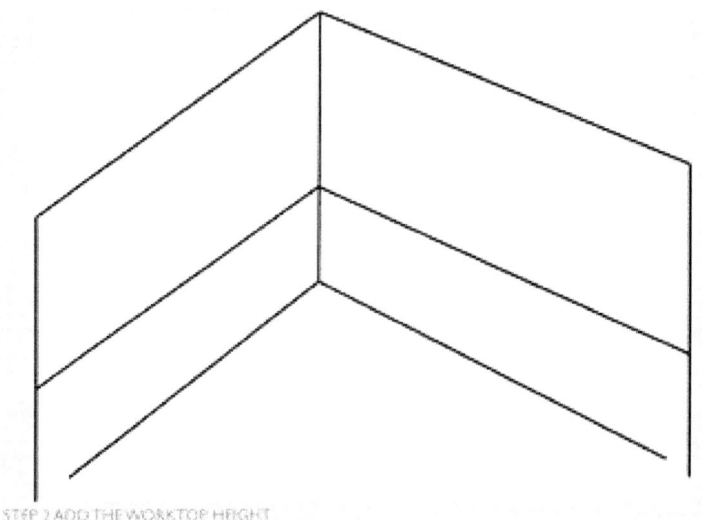

STEP 2 ADD THE WORKTOP HEIGHT

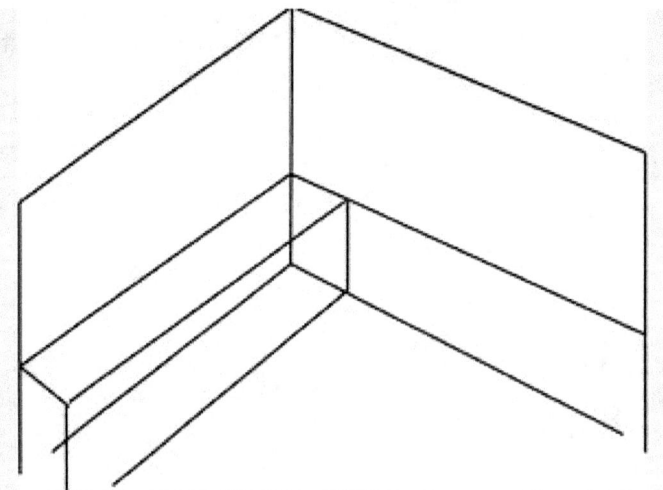

STEP 3 - ADD THE FULL CARCASE OUTLINE OF THE LH BASE UNITS

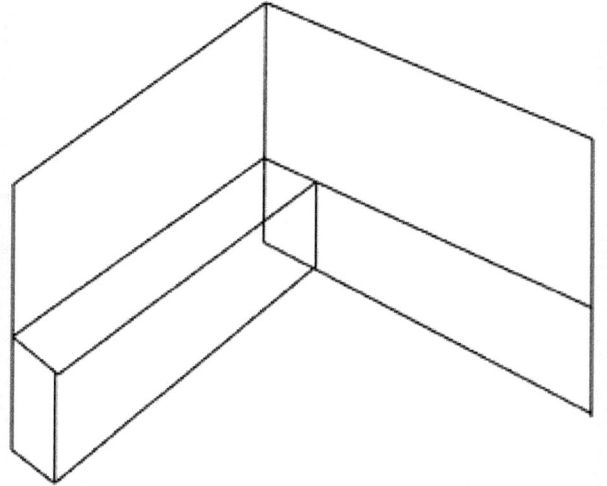

STEP 4 - TIDY UP THE OUTLINE AND UNFINISHED LINES

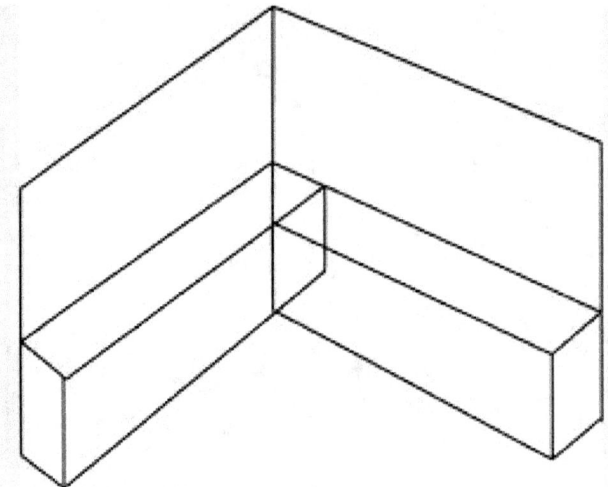

STEP 5 - ADD THE UNITS ON THE RH SIDE

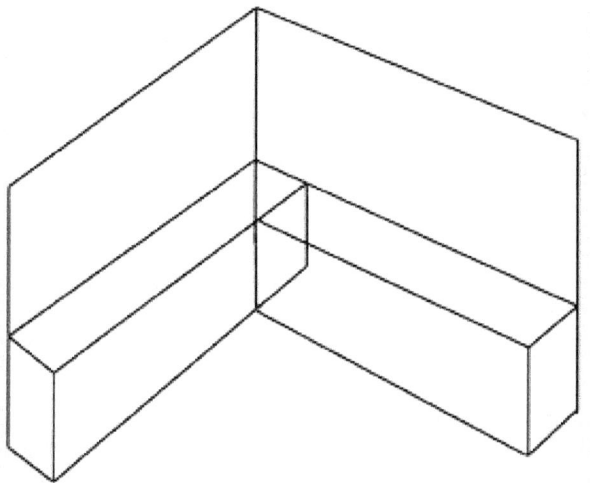

STEP 6 - AT THIS STAGE YOU CAN PROCEED WITH ADDING DOORS, WORKTOP THICKNESS, PLINTH LINES AND OTHER DETAILS IF YOU WISH

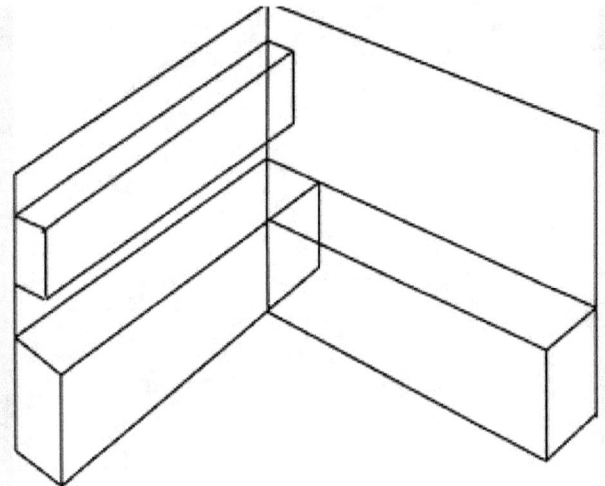

STEP 7 - ADD THE WALL LINE - ON THIS PLAN ALL WALL UNITS ARE ON LH

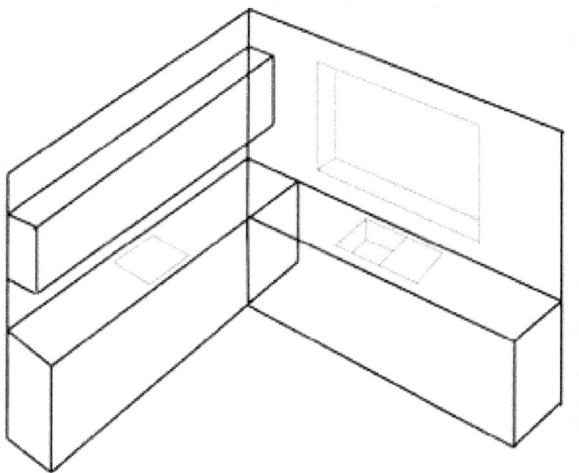

STEP 8 - AT THIS STAGE YOU CAN COMPLETE OTHER DETAILS SUCH AS THE WINDOW, HOB, SINK, ETC.

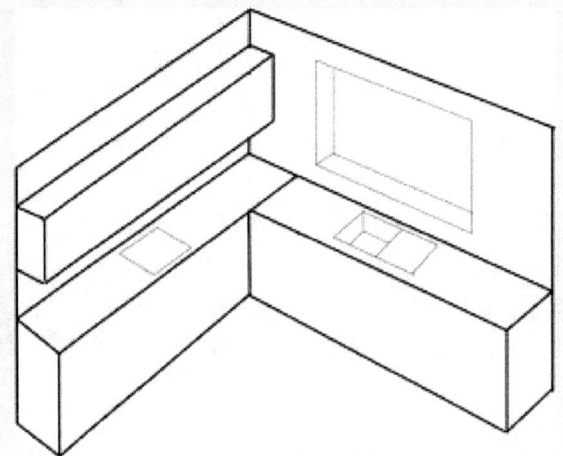

STEP 9 - TIDY UP THE OUTLINE REMOVING HIDDEN LINES ETC.

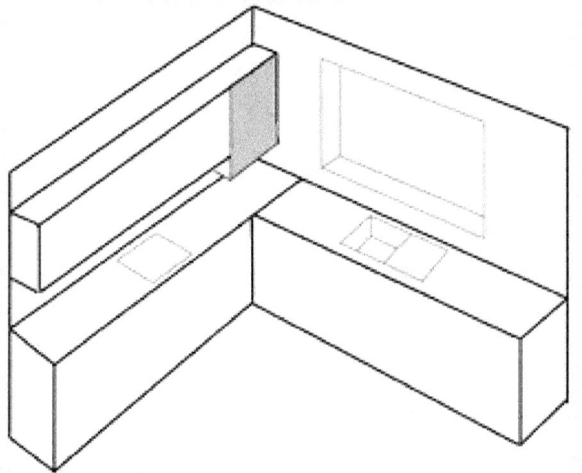

STEP 9B - optional - There is an error on the wall line , you could add a display unit at the end which will hide the error - plus at this stage you could add other details

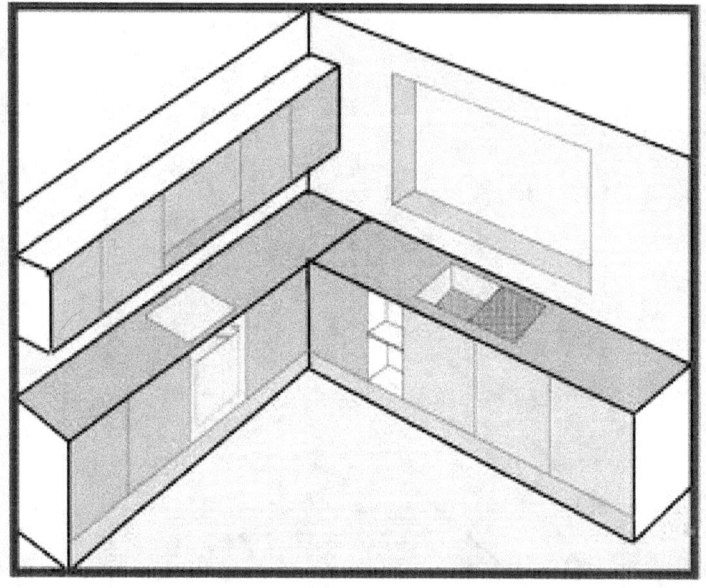

Final stage rendering as desired.

4

Using a Computer

Almost everyone has a computer but not a drawing board in the 21st century.

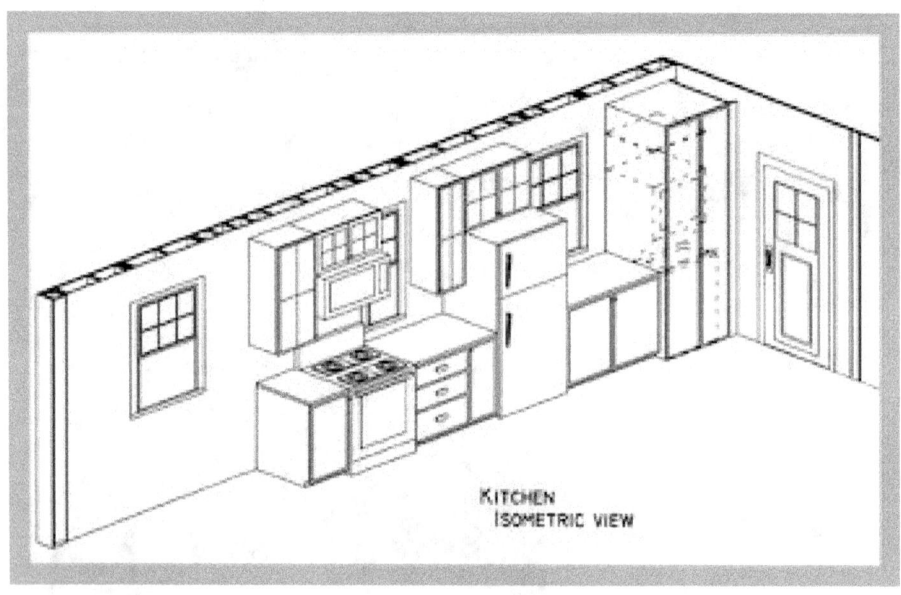

KITCHEN
ISOMETRIC VIEW

So if you would like to use the facilities on your computer - no problem. It is slightly trickier at first but with just a little practice the technique is easily developed. There are many FREE drawing programmes out there for both Mac and PC. Many of the programmes also have an angle restriction so you can set your angles. If not use a simple protractor at first and then you will be able to simulate the angles at will.

For the first few start of with pencil and paper drawing just to familiarise yourself with the technique and you can then move on to your computer programme probably after trialling just a couple of drawings

Most programmes have a simple 90° restriction for perfect vertical and horizontal lines so that part is built in. If your programme does not have angle restriction use a protractor for the first attempts and then you will gradually become used to the angles and be able to guestimate their positioning. Funnily enough when you get into real perspectives the lines are easier to draw on the computer as you have a vanishing point reference.

Thank you

Well I hope you have enjoyed this Mini Guide experience and perhaps you will join us again in another of these Guides. Please remember that the portrait guides are simpler and therefore cheaper than the landscape guides and the planning guides will vary because of the graphic content but the aim is always to produce an inexpensive and convenient guide.